AS BEST W‸ CAN

Jeffrey Wainwright was born in Stoke-on-Trent and educated locally and at the University of Leeds. He taught American Studies at the University College of Wales Aberystwyth and for a year (1970-71) at Long Island University, Brooklyn, NY. In 1973 he moved to Manchester Polytechnic, later Manchester Metropolitan University, from where he retired as Professor of English in 2009. In 1984 he was Judith Wilson Fellow at St John's College Cambridge. He has translated Charles Péguy, Paul Claudel, Pierre Corneille and Bernard-Marie Koltès for the RSC, the BBC and the Actors' Touring Company. He was northern theatre critic for *The Independent* newspaper for eleven years. His literary criticism includes *Acceptable Words: Essays on the Poetry of Geoffrey Hill* (MUP) and *Poetry the Basics* (Routledge). Jeffrey Wainwright lives in Manchester and for part of the year in Umbria.

Also by Jeffrey Wainwright, from Carcanet

What Must Happen
The Reasoner
Clarity or Death!
Out of the Air
The Mystery of the Charity of Joan of Arc (Tr.)
The Red-Headed Pupil
Selected Poems
Heart's Desire

JEFFREY WAINWRIGHT

As
Best
We
Can

CARCANET

ACKNOWLEDGEMENTS

Some of these poems have appeared in *PN Review*, *Stand* and the
Times Literary Supplement. Thanks for criticism and encouragement
to my indefatigable editor Michael Schmidt and all at Carcanet
and to Jon Glover, Robert Gray, J. J. Healy, John Lancaster, Alf
Louvre, John McAuliffe, Judith Wainwright and John Whale.

First published in Great Britain in 2020 by
Carcanet
Alliance House, 30 Cross Street
Manchester M2 7AQ
www.carcanet.co.uk

A CIP catalogue record for this book is
available from the British Library.

ISBN 978 1 78410 988 2

Book design by Andrew Latimer
Printed in Great Britain by SRP Ltd, Exeter, Devon

The publisher acknowledges financial
assistance from Arts Council England.

CONTENTS

to J.J. 'Jack' Healy

AS BEST WE CAN

GIVE ME A LINE

Give me a line, any line will do,
it could feature for instance
this periwinkle blue,
it could make a start.

Or I could attend this magpie
on the ledge, he is brisk, fears little,
is at home on brick as much as grass,
he has his place and might be understood.

I like to think that we can make a start
from here, or indeed from anywhere,
you and I, at figuring why we are,
like all else, just so, enabled

to talk and touch, argue and kiss
until we shall be separated,
the world scarcely needing to adjust
as we are so differently disposed.

THE OTHER POEM

Empty windows, empty balconies,
clouds that seem desultory,
only the tree-tops shuffle slightly
in a light wind,
birds go by too fast for the scene.

Nothing else to describe.
Should I lift my head?
Might there be something
to entertain you
over the ledge and in the street below?

The sea is close by –
as it says in the other poem –
but here it is really true.
The sea is a wall it says,
But that I cannot confirm.

I could seek out the gulls
and watch them alight,
taking their nodding
as they walk for greeting,
but that would be fanciful.

The wind from the sea
is now grand and slow –
but that too is from the other poem.
Truthfulness may be all.
I just want a sound I might add in.

SIGNS OF LIFE

on the evergreen continent
a buzz-saw or a sander,
a series of aircraft processing into cloud,
birds intent and attent caw and call,
flowers bloom past convolvulus,

all 'signs of life', making time

trees have grandeur, nothing less,
cicadas stopping and starting in unison,
spiders risking all,
some wrapping-paper blown about the street,
a baker riding pillion home.

SPRING WALK

It is nondescript this long pond,
ignored, left to itself.
The rushes, still straw-yellow
in the early Spring, have maintained
their tenancy, a can and a gin-bottle
disturb them not. They thrive.

Among them, just visible
in ripple and shadow, their cawks
sometimes audible, frogs pursue
their ends: nutriment, spawn,
year into year.

And life can be less than this,
a silverfish on a bathroom tile,
rosettes of lichen plastered on stone,
other mites immobile or invisible.

It seems there is nothing lifeless,
nothing that dares not strive,
nothing that is not open to its death.

IN THE ARMS OF THE TREE

the arms of the cherry-tree certainly beseech,
but what is the point of that?
why plant ourselves inside a common tree?

the people lift their arms to heaven, and perhaps a dove,
their blue sleeves fall back,
they beseech as modelled by what they know

sleeves are the conjuror's stock-in-trade
but the cherry-tree in question
practises neither magic nor sleight of hand

though something here is confusing longing
with the blueness of some clothes
and what might be seen in the posture of a tree.

THE PLAN

A white towel on a washing-hoist
bearing some blurred shadows.

This is but one thing occurring
within the folder of the day,
and of the continent,
and of as far as we can think.

And of course I am watching it now,
liking how the shadows
pause and surge, agitate and swoon,
focus briefly then slide off the edge.

But I am committed also
to common thought
and so am bound to ask how come this,
or anything, is occurring.
What *is* the plan?

The hoist moves left then right,
two steps one way and two the other,
gracefully, like a dancer in the old tyme –
and there comes a likeness barging in,
convinced only likenesses recruit consequence.

Which might do for now and hereabouts
but what is the plan?

THE SWIRL

Am I lost here, as is so often said?
I stand beneath trees I cannot understand,
among rocks that stay closed,
among birds whose styles are quite beyond me.

The painter paints a prospect all his own,
but without trees, only bald arcades and porticoes.
For him at least the swirl is paused.
He knows which way to turn to take his walk.

And that is science! – a way to get by
out in the woods or among the stones,
knowing nothing of them beyond description
but at least which way is up or out.

Words, signals, signs leave naught to go on,
even what was kept from us erased,
until the roofbeam dries to a tinder-crack,
and the lean-to depends less and less,

THE IDEA

Only the sky grey and watery,
little else comes into view,
a tranche of the tree still leafless,
a purple pot upturned,
all bounded by the window-frame.

I am looking for an idea,
something that can connect
these different things –
there are enough of them! –
and will justify me.

But it wants to be left
where it may not be, unspoken,
between this segment of the tree
and the upturned pot,
now less purple than it was before.

THIS WINDOW AGAIN

I'm looking out of this window again.
There is a cabbagy pot-plant
hunkering down for winter, other pots
are empty, rummaged by squirrels.
The trees are starting to bear the marks,
or scars, of autumn and I am up against
meaning once more – is there something
out there on the lawn or am I bound
to make up whatever I will believe
is to be found in a tree or season?

Let me not look outside today, but ignoring the lightwell,
the lawn, the tree and all the world outside and what
it might mean, look just at my window-ledge
and its horse-brass screwed into a wooden base;
the tea-bell chased with indistinct Egyptian scenes,
its tinkly clapper long gone probably; a dromedary
kneeling, patient, loaded and ready to rise,
a 'ship of the desert'; and three monkeys
insisting they will see, hear and speak no evil,
all these things the last of the brasses we had at home,
'done' in those days, that is polished, weekly.
Then there is a photo of me perhaps aged 4, smiling nicely
in a white vyella blouse, its plastic frame
no bigger than some foreign postage-stamp
and next to that a tin compass, simple enough
but still able to tell me I am facing south.
More colourful, a china model of Jemima Puddleduck
in her blue bonnet with the avuncular Mr Fox
in his brown waistcoat that Audrey gave me
before she lost her mind - fine work from Beswick's
Beatrix Potter collection of the kind she did herself,
and then two late photographs of my Mum
who in latter days found Audrey a good and cheerful friend.
In one she is raising a glass, not really her
but she *is* at Tom's wedding, in the other she is in her chair
with those two long red candles that were never lit
on the shelf behind.   There is another photo of her
with my Dad sitting, I think, near the seaside,
tarpaulined boats in the background,
his arm round her shoulder and both of them
looking so happy.   What else?   My only

sporting trophy, Longton Schools Cricket Cup 1954
with Florence Primary and my name incised,
and a plaster William Shakespeare seated.
Sundry other photos: the children playing
water-games in Grandad's garden. That in colour,
and Dad in black and white and tie and pullover
looking away from the camera as advised, and
my mother, my wife, my daughter all together.
That old rectangular wind-up clock in green bakelite
always showing half-past eight, morning or night.
Morning or night is what I see beyond the lightwell,
morning then night, morning then night.

IF ALL THIS DID BEGIN

How beautiful our blue-marbled planet from afar,
and so serene, so steady as she goes,
escape-velocity nicely tailored to permit
philately, football and sales of work.

The lizard's silence is not a prayer but is a stratagem.
Likewise warbling of every suit,
a chameleon ambush, the stoat's removal
of her kits, the finery of meadow grass.

The cardsharp of the riverboat saloon
begets descendants, further connoisseurs
of the shortest odds, then a diligent cashier,
perhaps an ever-optimistic therapist.

If all this did begin how might it go on?
And might some understanding, yet to be achieved,
as differently abled as a snake or whale,
recognise a willing purpose and a gracious end?

GREETINGS

I

Good morrow brother louse
(commonest of wood-lice).
Are you content enough
among these paving-stones?
The great star has just
stepped away
and the moon, so self-effacing,
is backing gently
into the light.
Do you need to know this
for your purposes,
and what might they be?
Of course I could research them.
They must include nutriment
for sure, what will keep
your tiny armour
metalled enough,
and your stolid pursuit energised
for as long as necessary –
I note there are fewer of you
abroad today.
But only the sky has control
and might in some form remain
and prove eternal.

2

Good morrow Senhor.
Are you really a lizard
for these parts?
You seem longer than you might
and your kind of green,
virtually viridian,
could draw down
an unwelcome stare.
But here you stand,
motionless
but for the small stomp
of your neck pulse,
sizing up your situation
and what should be
your next serious move.
How much of this attention
are you bound to pay
for safety
and advancement?
This is I'm sure
the same stone universe
wherein we find ourselves.
How like and like
is what it asks of us?

3

My questions are
what they have to be,
as addressed to lice or lizards,
a little pretence
cranking the rhetorical.
I need also speak to clouds
assuming nothing else
will answer,
as though believing
they will tell me true
how we are
under this local sun,
crouched at a table
or stretched on a low divan
and under instruction
from every galaxy
alive and dead.
Thank heavens
that these pink flowers
balanced
on their slender stems,
these plums,
gripping the tree,
can almost be described.

4

... 'can almost / be described',
by mugging up on pistils,
or through such words
as might be beautiful,
though with nothing of the flower?
But neither will forestall
the remorseless re-wind
into questions.
And how proud is this mind
to see these things invisible,
the knowing coils
it can find to grapple with,
heaving itself
above the unworthy ruck –
'Look I am good at this,
I really am!
And I exist!'
That lizard I have not seen again,
the wood-lice are past their season,
clouds come and go –
so why should I care for them,
they are no more than presences.
What I can entertain is here,
far beyond the nameless stars.

5

Unless – is this a threat
or a promise? – *unless*
we already know what is
the only real abstraction.
This mind will go
its long way round,
fancying the eternal
lies in perfect circles
and the no-name god,
devising every kind of dazzle
to believe it can confuse
death's set coincidence
and scratch itself
a toe-hold in eternity,
but only side-steps
what hides before us.
Death is what it is, stupid,
nothing more
philosophical than that.
We are as palpable
as the lizard, louse
and cloud with whom –
must I say? – we can
almost be described.

THE LAKE

The red slipper of the dawn steals across
the line of hills, its confidence today
just as before. Hard to understand how
it might seem tentative as it captures
and lights the waiting lake. The whole day
then stirs, shrugs and follows suit.

*

The lake stands there between the trees,
even behind the trees, out of sight, but
still there – of course it is, whether grey or
blue, it stands there to reason. Does something
stipulate that there is knowledge of this
kind, something inscrutable yet plain?

*

The weather breathes upon the lake.
Suddenly everything is beautiful
especially that distant inlet
and the white boat with its fisherman.
He proceeds inwards, beyond my sight,
his landfall surely embraced by trees.

*

It is to one side and well below where
my mind sits and stares at the darker patch
on the farther shore which was yet darker
and a different green. But now that patch
is lost. A cloud-shadow is all it was, though
it seemed so anchored in the noble scene.

*

I was looking for a face or sign upon
the waters' flat impassive span
but there's nothing – an unconscious
cloud-shadow, nothing notable, only
obedient part-work, sad creature
of the casual battlements above.

*

Imagined as bodies for the umpteenth time,
these shadows on the wood
seem 'dragonish', imperious,
exhaling themselves proudly across
the humble trees before vanishing
piecemeal, nonchalant, unconcerned.

*

The significance of the lake falls away
so strive to hasten it as it goes,
tear from its false countenance
the last vestment and last humour
fetched from afar to colour in
its brazen vacancy.

*

Ah these 'many states of the soul'
hard by the margins of the lake.
Gaura and willow-herb might be confused
by an unpractised eye. Neither
belongs here. Nor these deadheaded roses
flickering into further bloom.

*

Now here comes the thunder and whatever
it is saying nowadays, barrels
rolling downstairs towards us in the vaults
or caverns of a children's story.
The lake absorbs it all, lightning included,
and needs not even brace itself for harm.

*

A dead tree still standing high above
the lake is a solemn, and a sorry sight.
But it is the martins' misericord, where they rest
from their frantic labours, climbing and diving
in the speck-laden air, their lake of fishes,
their high veldt of game, their ocean shoals.

*

Across the other side six poplars
stand sentinel by the shore.
Upright, military, their being is surely
all martial, just as their opaque cousin
cypress holds death
deep inside its dense and wary heart.

*

In full sun, at midday, the lake is not
at its best, its colour is uniform,
leaden, every kink in the shore
readily there and nothing given
to mystery, beholden to no incident
nor sensing anything incipient.

*

Shrink-wrapped hay-bales glint above the shore,
their shine part of the sun's work at this hour,
as are stray windscreens and sun-roofs
whose owners are shaded somewhere, botanising
perhaps, or tidying their samples
and paperwork for calls this afternoon.

*

There is no signal on the surface here
though currents must ride through open doors below.
Some conditions will bring driftwood
into view, each piece finding other debris
to form slow rafts that seem piloted
towards the patient shore.

*

Of point and purpose: how intelligible
is the lake? Its irrigations are the reason
for the village drowned but what of
its colours and misshapen mists,
need these be understood?
How daring must the mind be now?

*

I've not heard, nor heard of, any church-bell
beneath the water, nor of anyone old
tied to a chair as the waters rose.
Perhaps there was a cat stuck up a tree
out of earshot. All else decamped to higher ground
leaving so much to a different world.

*

No flesh-footed shearwater fetches up here –
wrong salination, wrong trade-winds,
wrong hemisphere divided east and west.
Even so-called local gulls pass this lake
which means that, being unfrequented,
I can make it lonely and so sorrowful.

*

Ocean waves must beat upon the shore,
they cannot turn aside. They are raging
to be free but hopelessly. The drowsy lap
lap at the shelving of the lake never seems
agitated or ill-at-ease but is content
to live as it lives. It has found its bond.

*

Still. Stillness. Why do we, who must move
to live, hanker so much for tranquillity?
Why do we want the lake to be 'like glass',
for there to be 'no breath of air'?
Stillness is the chamberlain sent on ahead –
we should racket and bang our pots and pans.

*

Some tiny figures, seemingly in black
from here, patrol the farther shore.
What might be washed up for them?
A single plimsoll will be no use
and only the rarest bottle or ancient shard.
The lake's gift is their expectation.

*

An aircraft that can't be seen grinds
its way above the lake, finding,
before it passes on, some regard
of what it sees below, the lake's whole shape,
its interesting, haphazard outline
that I so long to see entire.

*

I want to find some pattern in the lake,
something in twelves since that is what
I was given early to fit around the world –
the shilling, the Apostles, inches to the foot.
But it will not do, nor any crystal shape.
Nothing straight-edged can resolve the scene.

*

I watch the lake between the trees,
its sheen goes silvery in the evening light.
How much it changes and so challenges
these quite capable and hard-working words
leaving them wan and out of sorts.
Not so much has been achieved.

*

Dusk. Along the skyline a lemon-yellow
sunset turning orange. A solitary light,
high in the trees, comes on, the first to ward off
the fearsome dark. Then others follow,
clutching at their own relief
until only the lake is blackness.

BELVEDERE

Even up here we cannot think we see it all.
Trees, grass, haze, vines, a bird
hastening horizontally across,
and so many creatures and human things holed up:
a badger that will be abroad tonight,
a stone fountain dried out and overgrown.

I could begin again with other instances:
the nearly-yellow track angled against the wood,
a snail clutching the iron footing of a post,
unrippled water on the lake,
a stationary boat in silhouette,
closer by, some friendly human murmuring.

Yet we keep the will to understand it all.
We watch the wireworm and the humming-moth
as best we can; study the undersoil;
figure river-tides and how they might be tamed;
invent gradations to suit the way we see,
but still are pestered by so much profusion.

So what we do is make this stand for this,
as representative, pretending there is enough of
every single tree to make it one with
every other single tree despite a shivered branch,
or whatever stance it offers to
the awkward sky. We must do this

or be swept away – fixing that single name inside
our careful and uncoloured mind
as the clearest beauty we can know.
But life is there only in every separate thing,
each flutter of a dream near the edge of sleep.
We would not wish less of ourselves to be recognised.

DREAMS OF LENNOX ROAD

Lennox Road is always in my dreams.
Lila, winning a race, scudding over the grit
and puddles, is always on Lennox Road
though she has never been there, knows nothing of it.
It is my dream alone, though surprisingly hospitable.
It holds me, clasps me to itself
as though, independent as it seems, it has need of me.
Lennox Road, the place and name, always in my dreams.

\#

'You're walking well today,' I say, drawing level.
It's uphill, but not too steep, it's Chaplin Road.
He smiles but does not speak. I take his arm.
Perhaps it is his shoes, white plimsolls
and three pairs of socks, the last one white
and turned over. His duffel coat is from 1965,
black and only done up half-way.
We stop where I turn off for Lennox Road.
He must carry on up, on his researches.
It is Lilian Gish that he must find he says.

\#

How can you belong here?   The dream says we are
in Lennox Road but you and it are not quite right,
though the margin out the back, some grass, garages,
fruit-canes and an entryway could be that particular ground.
Were you waiting there for me to come near the back-door,
perhaps to put something out, so that I would see you
overflowing that child's chair in a voluminous
and confusing dress?   You were nearly an enemy
but you're smiling now, though I'm still uncertain
and don't know whether to approach or speak.
And who are you beckoning to as though off-stage,
and are you saying 'Look, here he is'?

#

I'll need a taxi home from here.
I ask him 'Take me to Ch… Ch… Chaplin Road.'
There it is in my mind's eye with a map
but I know that's not where I go now, going home.
But nothing else, no other name will appear…
Ch… Ch… Ch… Chaplin Road… until
slowly it clears and is replaced by now.

#

Clothes all over the floor, shirts, ties, trousers, underwear,
as though drawers have never been filled.
It feels like it must be the wrong dream,
an image perhaps from some book I've read,
but no, it insists, this is Lennox Road indoors,
but with nothing familiar, no view, no window,
but still it insists, this is Lennox Road.

\#

Yes, this is Lennox Road again,
from the back garden this time,
and from the rockery end,
his back to the house, an Australian
is bowling and I am quite confident.
But the ball takes my hip or bat-handle
and I am caught for naught.
Back up the rockery steps I go
and one who is sitting chewing
says nothing as I go past.
They are wearing maroon caps
but this is an Ashes Test!

\#

We are the chosen venue!
For the closing event, the final jamboree!
Crowds of everyone are here
and along Deggs' path next door
children from schools process
with flowers in their hair and holding hands.
The dignitaries are taking their place
above the garden, all looking slightly Edwardian
a few wing-collars, somewhere a silver band.
I am the MC, standing up on our back step
but such is the acclaim no word is required.
Geoffrey steps forward – it is like the opening
of a public park or railway – he starts to read.
A tear shows in his eye.

\#

no dreams of Lennox Road for months now

in this other world my father was first to leave
exasperated and beginning to panic that afternoon
(a nurse noted that shaking her head)
and he was gone that very same night

then my mother, *piano piano* through weeks
of who knows what kind of sleep
or wakefulness, until one afternoon, out of the sun
she slid away, leaving her body
which carried on changing anyway

so there are all my indwellers of Lennox Road
departed, pencil-shavings caught in the air,

though they might or might not re-appear
in the random play of dreams

my brain bringing them along, an occasional reflex,
perhaps a gift, but in some guise
not of their choosing nor of mine

\#

this is Lennox Road, that I know,
though it is the other end
where we are playing on the bricks
and the device we have is not working

it is a box but the numbers
on each of its screens flicker
and turn themselves back to front,
it is broken, finished, irreparable,
we cannot play though this time
I don't know who we are

then – just like that – one says
'I'll go and get another'
and yes, there at the end of the street
is Pye's sweet and lolly shop,
Mrs Pye with her big refrigerator,
and here in this dream she had one in
and someone brings it back with only
this afterthought of coins
and we settle on the kerb again

#

again at the other end
amid the old houses
I have an address but I'm not sure
and I knock on a door
no answer
but next door responds
and it is Dorothy whom I seek,
she does not look like her
but it is, I can see

just then the other door
opens a space,
an old lady there though she stays
behind the door, not speaking,
I try to explain
she stays in the dark of her house
I look to Dorothy
and am at a loss

#

I'm at the other end, the old houses
and the poorer end
and my friend (whom I do not recognise)
goes to her friend's to ask for me
if she knows

she comes to the door, friendly,
and asks us in over the broken step
(I wonder where is the man who should fix this?)
there is a child too
and the house is all for her
on every wall
on every surface
and hanging from the ceiling
are toys and decorations
soft toy chimps, teddies and dolls,
plastic games, bagatelles,
an irrepressible jack-in-a-box
that seems alive and must be
stuffed into a wall repeatedly

\#

I wake in my old room
though I know I am grown-up now
and I just know I am alone here

I lurch out of bed
and with but one mis-step
get to the door
and to the bathroom
where the bath is as I remember it
but the toilet bowl not
until the room is filled in
as by a sketch-pencil working fast
an invisible help

\#

We have finished our training
and somebody and I hit the New York streets
as drummers, door-to-door salesmen
of TV Sport packages.

George is first to answer the door,
he has glasses and smiles warmly.
'But what I would like,' he says,
is a package for theatre and the arts.'
'That can be arranged,' I say.
'I live close by, I can bring you
the brochure information that you need.'
'Thank you,' says George, 'I'll wait for it.'

And I go back to the street
which is Lennox Road for sure.

#

This is strange.   It's been a fast trip home,
five hours by car, but from Australia.
We draw up outside No. 10,
parking under the gaslamp.
A woman in a straw hat, not our sort, with a child
is walking down our path
passing through the garden it seems,
used to it since we have been away.
Then we – who are 'we'? –
are indoors but next door, in Deggs' house, No. 12,
looking out of their window.
And where are they?

\#

Pedalling 'furiously'
I turn the corner into Chaplin Road,
slightly uphill,
and it is suddenly slow going,
the brake-blocks
are sticking on the rims
more and more
till I drag to a stop
foundering.
Lennox Road is still up there ahead.
I won't make it back there now.

\#

This one is different.
I have flown home to check everything is ok.
I am at the back door of Lennox Road
at first hard shut.
Then I can open it into that scullery
and our old dog that never lived there.
Everything is in order into the living room.
All as it should be.

#

We stop to take a photograph
but as we do a yellow taxi
corners at speed, almost on two wheels
with the rest of our gang hanging out the windows
laughing and cheering
on the way to the war.
And yes, it is Bengry's shop
on the corner, the corner of Lennox Road.

DRAWING LESSONS
after John Ruskin

'Now if you can draw that stone, you can draw anything'
The Elements of Drawing

for Brian Maidment

*

look your stone antagonist boldly in the face

I do. I mean, *I try*. I falter but do not fall back.
I will valiant be! It is not my pencil,
nor my hand but the bounds of my attention
that have no membraned stuff tough enough.

How does a stone wait for us? At the ready?
Why does it antagonise so? Resistant
to all entreaty, obduring, yet what might
it relieve us of? What could it pillage?

Then why must I stand up, why try to seize
and satchel the likeness of a stone?
Is this how to live on the earth about us,
believing a stone is honoured by a line?

A stone, a leaf, their fragile shadows clinging –
we are not of them however proximate they seem.
And yet 'their fragile shadows clinging'
will adhere. How do I muster a tender act?

the best drawing-masters are the woods and hills

You are my best drawing-masters, you and your kin
and I am instructed. But does my pencilling
bring me towards a sight of you,
even to a glimpsing, the moon inside a cloud?

Everything is human, nothing looks itself:
the leaf is sorrow bent, the willows
cradle-arch the headlong stream,
the waters either errant or stymied in their pools,

the trees clustered but still unneighbourly,
even you, old stone, junk from a hapless cliff,
are harried and beset,
made but to serve my cognizance.

O tree, stone, air, babbling brook, will you not be yourself!
I see you sometimes strolling sometimes spry,
but only ever as you are not, captured
again and again just so, but nothing like.

dense and unmalleable this world

Dense and unmalleable this world indeed,
so what is to be done? Stories try to
hoick it into order, patting it like butter
or a brick, something to put a finger on,

a dish or a flight of consequences.
But how do they end? vain loves and fruitless deaths.
The pencil line at least is modest, no exhilaration,
often a wholly grey or rainy day is best.

In such a light tree-boughs stand like dark rivers
against the sky, the sky like long-fallen snow,
and I'm trying again at my spiny conker-shells:
can I get them to split upon the page?

Oh my scuffed, rubbed, dirtied patient page,
there seems nothing between the world and you
but in some shape it stays out there.
Is there a tender point, a tender thought to move it?

mew and howl

mew and howl how much indeed do I mew and howl,
not for the drudgery of shading but for the whole
codge-modge I am making –
the lines off-beam, the shadowing

too profound, the volumes pancake-flat,
and as I rub and rub and try again
the stale bread I use scratches and maims
this smudged, fingerprinted and dishonest page

and crumbles about the room. Yet I must go slow!
I know that the swish of a line drawn
with what is called freedom is wrong,
as leaving bread to waste upon a window-sill

is wrong, that I should never let my natural hand
think it might go free, that hereabouts is nothing
but itself. Better the codge-modge, I'm thinking.
I cannot be God, not even on a page.

Nature will show you nothing if you set yourself up for her master

And why not, pal? How much poke does she think she has?
Look at these naïve potato-flowers,
so silly, so virginal, they are bound to look my way,
the orange-tree, for all its spikes, cannot act

rebarbative enough. Turves, a slouching hare,
another sunless copse, fields without folk,
the charcoal tumble of a mountain stream,
a makeshift grotto in the rocks above,

my cross-hatched lilies, all these stand there,
dutiful and still, not an itch not a twitch.
For Nature has nothing new to show,
nothing unanticipated, unforeseen,

unmined and unrefined, nothing my stylus
cannot incise, nothing unbidden by guile
or charm or force. I am set up,
a master and bestride; Nature moonstruck, daft.

shutting the light gradually up (i)

The faintest of lines drawn across the page
sets this process off; a bucket of pitch,
a broad brush, heavy-laden, becomes logical,
and we see the end of art is blackness.

So what now? Thankfully, some strides are easy,
especially in thought, and just one
will take us to the Half-Way House
licensed for the sale and consumption

of alcoholic beverages in some full name
always neatly legible beneath the transom
of etched or frosted glass. Inside, the varnished
wood is styled in brushed horizontal strokes

and everywhere there are circles to be seen,
coins, beermats, stools, fixings of many sorts
and hues and patterns in clothes, labels, skin.
Though never untouched, light does pass.

shutting the light gradually up (ii)

Meanwhile, back at the artists' camp, the light had changed.
Was this a 'trick', a variation of the variation
slyly declined from its routine pilgrimage?
Light holds so many options it can ignore habit,

and even though we artists exult in this
we cannot keep up – now we see it now we
see it otherwise.   Loosed from the sun
light turns us without mercy or regard,

so many particulars, special cases, glimpses left aside:
that's a dry leaf scurrying not a snake or a shrew,
a tree cut off against a now truncated sky,
a weir-stone turning its water into perfect glass.

Weary of this we are, just like the mythic soul
who journeyed on in timeless and perpetual light
until she sat, closed her eyes, and shutting the light
gradually up, gave us the darkness and the night she
dreamed.

there's a line and a natural line

there's a line and a natural line
but what you will ask of course is how
anyone can be that definite. The line defines
is all I can say, which is convenient.

In latitudes where the sky is lineless
you can wait all day to limn a cloud-edge.
Swing-ropes tautened by a broken seat
hang there as stand-ins, their twinings and plaitings

made natural by gravity you could say,
a convenience that I imagine as
stair-rods, cartoon rain, lines heading straight down
something as natural as you can get.

But the bough curves upwards and the hand
strives to follow it, leaps to think that it has found
the natural line and cries out boldly:
'Look, we are as one! Me and this patient tree!'

there was a spacious half of seat vacant in my little hooded carriage

Verticals, horizontals, diagonals, antagonists all.
A line that ought to be approaching neatly
saunters suddenly aside, takes the perspective
so the void collapses and the space is lost.

The paper neither smiles nor scowls, an ice-dive
could find no mischief there however deep it is.
I could arraign the always-otherness
of natural things like the four pines across

the near-horizon, five when I look again.
Yet all the world out there demands is some attention.
Four or five? That at least. They even stand
stock still this morning as though to be of help.

Snow falls on the river and is then something else.
On some scaffolding that man in a high-vis tee
must watch his step. Better his foot does not find
a gangplank changing into vacant air.

…creatures who are every instant perishing …

… creatures who are every instant perishing …
like a waterfall: there and at the same time vanishing;
always ellipsed but always with us.
They leave me tongue-tied but never leave.

Because what is instantly helpful to creatures
who are every instant perishing is …
revolving this is a regular shame.
Let me be helpful, in pencilling and elsewhere.

I draw a bar tightly across a page
and set to work. To one side
I scribble and scribble to a coalhouse black
and then seek to shade stealthily

toward the other side, greyer and lighter
with every touch into the page's patient white.
Dissatisfaction with what I do is wholesome, but I might
graduate to show some creature in the twilit sky.

the best answerer of questions is perseverance

The beauty of the light needs not to be
attested to, it boils and shudders anyway,
so to see things in themselves is to possess
composition enough – that can be securely said.

But then the gusts of sunlight unman me,
even as I lift my eyes to meet it
line and mass dissolve again just as I
duck beneath the parapet.

To be so lost in it, feeling blind,
no more than scrabbling as though this world
were lightless and once more the pencil blunts,
breaks and even the page begins to snigger.

The best answerer of questions is perseverance,
That will not be of the saintly kind
but that through wind and weather, all I am allowed
to help me seek whatever waits inside the light.

it would be bad advice that made you bold

But what scares me is to be thought
pusillanimous – 'Da da dee da da!
What yer waiting for Wainy?'
and meanwhile here comes Big Ballsy

pounding down the slope, going hard for it,
the big doffer, up and over the brook and –
nearly makes it, he falls back on landing,
you can see he's wet through to his pants.

But he dunna care, he beats his chest, he's ready
for the Cabaret Voltaire and grabs a megaphone:
DOFFERCOCKSTERBROCKSTERDOO –
surely this is 'the language of Paradise'!

But Ballsy had gone about as fer as he could go
and took up his pen again. 'I never could bid
chaos welcome' he wrote, and I am daunted anew.
Labour on therefore courageously.

You will never love art well till you love what she mirrors better

… what she mirrors better. Is shadowing then
what she is about, and why we are so enamoured,
so very smit by colour and by sock-wool
figured from a herring's useful skeleton?

Perhaps, but this makes me drawn to devilry.
R's modest 'what' is of course venerable
Ma Nature, our mother even when she was only
glops, molt and flame, not the jovial dame

of ladysmock, author of zephyrs and the noble nod
of cedar, oak and lime, who preceded
and must take precedence, making us feel small
as even pismires are revealed as better organised.

This is not how I choose to be chastised.
When I seek the shadow what looks back is human,
as mutable as a leaf or the artist's eye,
which looks and then makes up what it sees.

WHAT AM I SEEING?

*'What sort of human, pre-eminently human feeling it is that loves
a stone for a stone's sake, a cloud for a cloud's.' – Ruskin*

(i)
Why are there trees and bushes in the snow?
I could ask a weathergirl – she knows which way the wind blows.
Whichever - they are easy to get at and easy to pass by.

Another kind of question is
why has the brush painted
'Trees and Bushes in the Snow'?
Or 'A Bowl of Fruit', especially without
its tell-tale, vacated sea-shell lying conveniently by?
Why go to all that trouble of painting it
when you can have the real thing easy as pie?
(Sometimes I like to call a pie a pie, or a pie.)

But it *is* possible to worry here.
Granted, 'A Bowl of Fruit' is not a bowl of fruit,
for it can be – especially if a touch discomposed –
colour freed from line, or lines strolling, or 'structure',
and thus even a piece of the true universe;
and it may not have to work hard
to take me out of myself in the same way as an arena
of shadow under a kitchen-chair
is a version of the snow-capped roof-tiles opposite,
or, as another house does when it casts a witch-shadow,
again in the snow, so that I ask myself
'What *am* I seeing? What is *also* there? What is *really* there?'
and 'is this a good question or should I fetch the apples and the pears?'

(ii)

After Guercino. 'The Assassination of Amnon'

Amnon cops it at table, plates, apples and pears tumbling.
A left-cross topples him,
exposing his neck and throat, a brown patch of shadow
pointing in a 'v' towards the breast-bone,
shading off upwards towards the temple
so that the cheek can be just paper
turned from the dagger that is already coming down
in the fist of the second guest, inked in dark
beneath the handle, and then the blade bare to light
as it reaches the scribbles of his hair
and the two days' growth pen-scratched beneath his chin.

I too want to see the world as an arrangement:
the tunic bucklings and seams as interruptions
of light and that light washed gently over
so that the armpit appears, then the dark head and beard,
the tip of the second dagger also heavily inked in
until out of the empty white come the two guests.

*

Except, upon further investigation, they are not guests
but servants, seconded from the work of beasts
to the work of men.   Here is the justice of it.

Amnon cops it, but what looks like treachery is,
we will understand, true recompense.
Amnon has raped his half-sister, the girl-child *Tamar*,
though, as she says, had he asked the king for her
the king would not have demurred,
but *Amnon* raped her and then hated her
and had his servant bolt the door against her.
Rent, weeping, ashes upon her head,
she goes to her brother *Absalom*, himself half-brother
to *Amnon*, who guesses right and says:
'Hold now thy peace sister: he *is* thy brother;
regard not the thing.'
And she goes in and the story leaves her,
And we do not know if this brawl of justice
ever comforts her, or why, truly,
Absalom sees to it that she is avenged;
or if it is justice the brush and pen wants to show
or movement in ink.
'Get the line and shade more tender':
As you see a stone so you see a man.

WHO WAS ST CHAD?

In memory of my mother

Did God speak to Nell the way
that Anselm heard Him clear?
From Sandford Hill it was hard
to imagine the court of Christ,
the air not rare enough
to let her through.

O Longton in your photographs,
marvelling at your famous ovens,
the bottles of smoke, the soot, the dirt,
the blackened bricks, the sun
lost to the long flame
and its buried fire.

Here Nell listened for the obscure
voice of God, assuming nothing.
She knew she must abide
this darkness, the salt-cloud
of unknowing rolling up
Anchor Road towards the fields above.

It's my guess God stayed mum,
no rapturous bang or wallop,
nothing seraphic, nothing
stigmatical like that visited
on gaunt, vision-ready girls
in mossy grottos far away.

Did she worry much that He stays
unseen, this nevertheless living God,
this puzzle-setter *than whom nothing
greater can be thought*... who is
*whatever it is better to be
than not to be* etcetera?

She did not nourish doubt –
how could she spare the time? –
though when her sister
mocked her for her churchy ways
she longed for a sign
that would shut her up for good.

Sid, her other half, liked
to argue the toss
that folk who went to church
were the better for it,
better occupied than Mrs H
off to their 'van every weekend.

Taking a bag of toffee-rolls
to Ray, now too breathless
to say 'thanks', that's a Sunday job,
not fixing up a deckchair
and then four pints in the *Sailors' Rest*.
Never went to church himself though.

Smoke, travail, the scratch edges
of biscuit-ware, the saggar-men
heavy-laden. Rising early
on Sundays grants an hour
separate from the rest
and with all those different words.

1908 a brickwork boom:
St Chad came out of the rain
at Adderley Green,
Hugh Bourne lustily
memorialised along Stone Road,
his hefty chapel brimful of folk.

The sidesman would say, though only
to himself, 'I'm an ordinary man,
just a man in socks,
but when I'm in here it's different,
I don't feel so described.
We should all feel that way.

'And there's good things on this earth:
bringing you clean and
well-wrapped up from the
Cottage Hospital.   Hard then
to think of sin and all that.
The serpent has to sleep betimes.'

'Why is there summat and not nowt?
Tha dustna know, but think
a' this. If we wasna here,
all on us, milling rind,
He'd have no reason to exist.
It's Him depends on us.'

And they dug in and sang, all around
their work-space dirty with white dust,
chapel and church at odds
but both defiant against
time and motion. To the worthy world:
this is the Lord's day, not yours.

St Chad's always smelt too high
for most local tastes
but it was the scent of her girlhood,
a small touch of beauty,
a six-candle gleam,
all Father Cooper's parti-coloured copes.

Father Cooper, a mission priest,
though the 'heathenish estates'
came later, was the loveliest man.
He gave her a Shakespeare,
Warne's Chandos Classics much-prized,
not much read.   Was he the form of God?

Or at least the form of Man,
with a smile for you, not like men
must be on Sandford Hill, not like
her father, his innocent tobacco-knife,
his vengeful strap.   The priest
could listen, even to a girl.

It's him she remembers deep in
the Ordinary Time,
the yearly plod to Advent.
Through every dull Epistle
she remembers him and Chad's
silvery morns, the one bright spot.

Nell was a modest lady all her days
who always took her turn
to do the flowers,
iron the vicar's surplice,
vacuum all around. 'Drudgery divine'
she's heard it called, more than once.

She let herself in with the cleaner's key.
Closed inside that mysterious
diapered brick she liked the quiet.
The professors say the universe is silent
but with stars colliding there must be
something to be heard.   She listened.

Wherefore did we make a noise?
The band of the Boys' Brigade –
her brother Perce was a bugler in that,
he was chapel – drumming street
by street in springtime, the big lad
making his gladsome noise unto the Lord.

Or just enjoying himself.
Gladsome is how we should live,
even under judgement,
glad to know we can survive
without sting, without sighting
the orange fire unquenchable.

Gladsome we should be
even if we believe none of it,
should not be brazen
but gladsome in living as though –
as though there will be some
reckoning, some sort of quittance.

Some rapatag broke into church last night,
trashed it looking for cash
and left a steaming dump.
She cleaned it up of course
saying to herself
'Who knows where's sacred nowadays?'

The old tin chapel rusted to death.
The Prims' tabernacle, bathroom supplies.
Chad's hosts Weightwatchers on Wednesdays.
Who needed the Tuscan demi-columns
of St John's?   Dresden Methodist
New Connexion 'since demolished'.

'By the end there were only four of us
regular.   Harry and Philip had died
the same February and Ada said
she'll not come again unless
her son could drop her off – he'd not come
himself – why don't they these young folks?'

With the mighty Bourne now gone for
starter homes, its folk all in their heavens
somewhere beyond the Crem,
none of us these days worries much
where we are bound but click
and collect a longer life.

The preacher was right to rail
at rock 'n' roll. Bill Haley's
careful kiss-curl beckoned us
up stairways we'd never
dream dream dreamt about
and we just got shaken loose.

This is our modern life: first an inside lav.,
a motor-bike and sidecar,
then a smart saloon,
vaccinations against so much,
Reason lightens every load.
We don't need no story anymore.

Then it's all so frantic nowadays.
The big shop on Sundays,
get to the sales for school shoes,
sometimes a trip to Legoland.
These are not Vanities, we are not
living deliciously or waxing rich.

We do not love our kids the less.
We may be seen to check our phone
while grandma struggles for a word –
not in itself a mortal sin.
I'm sure any of us would cross over
to help a body fallen in the street.

But God we do not seek, early or late,
we thirsteth not nor longeth now it seems;
life's here and must be lived
somehow, making the best,
counsellors are often wonderful
and there are joys to be had.

Though how can we be the first
to live without the need
for pleas or prayers,
without imagining
a face in kindly stone – ,
or *summat* listening and taking heed?

By our vases do we mourn:
Dearest Grandad – Gone Fishing ...
reunited... locked in our thoughts.
Kleenex balled in every hand
we grieve to find the words
to measure up to measured death.

We want to know what's true here.
Is it all done with?
Was Perce but matter, a sister's love
never necessary, aimless,
tending to no end?
We need to know these things.

Nell had all the grand antitheses:
Though he were dead yet shall he live
though... worms destroy... yet in my flesh;
though and *yet* looked hard
and made their offering untrembling.
The thing, Death, nailed by common words.

Though she mourned yet was she comforted
though she was comforted yet did she mourn.
In words her God was nearly visible
perhaps there and everywhere.
She probed for Him most near Perce:
Was Christ there as he died she knew not how?

Was Perce, via the Boys' Brigade,
so comforted?   Knowing that,
she would have been so comforted
that Christ was by as someone sought
proper burial words to help
his soul past a false oblivion.

Or does Christ stop sometimes
by Longton Cenotaph on Trentham Road,
a ghost in his Light of the World garb
but still mortally unseen,
and invigilate awhile, though Perce
is absent from the roll?   God knows why.

Though she mourned yet was she comforted,
though she was comforted yet did she mourn
in her bedsit, behind her night-curtain.
Did she feel blessed, and so not alone?
What did those words do?
Who was St Chad, known to welcome rain?

What comes up when you google Death?
Not much.   Sites don't like to commit
beyond 'permanent cessation' and
'mystery'. There are quotes on 'Good Reads'.
Was it better to hearken to it weekly:
dust and ashes have no dominion?

I always wonder why I visit
ashes.   Clearly it makes no difference
to these long-gone bits of calx
as I stand here dutifully
once a year, an unbeliever.
They are gone but will not absent themselves.

They will persist, pursue us
'down the years'.   Or is it we
who mither them, striving
to drag them back to artificial light?
All that matters most is invisible.
Now we think that, now we don't.

Death as it appears to us
will not be solved, nor yet finessed.
Chad tried, Anselm tried, Nell tried
and though there is so much about us
that was once unseen, Perce and the angels
will not vouchsafe themselves.

Bodies chucked down slopes, bodies
never found, bodies reverently washed,
all dead, finished with.
And if the soul is there it slips
away, though still spoken of
as the word at the core of us.

Or else a piece of the body's
brainwork made (up)
to dignify its faecal dross,
a compliment we can't resist –
'we' not knowing what we are
any better than we know St Chad.

MY FATHER AND 'THE ONWARD TENDENCY'

Because he could not bid chaos welcome
he railed at me who made a botch of long-division.
Yet how could he not respect Arithmetic
when it had saved him from the pit,
from long days a mile under North Staffordshire,
familiar injuries, coal-veins from every cut and scratch?
Instead clean hands and nails, a trilby
and a decent gaberdine, his foolscap ledgers
without a blot or smudge safe every night.
It was not much, but better,
and if I could master long-division
and the rest I might be a Dr. Salk or another of the heroes
by whose deeds children are plucked
from iron lungs and fearsome calipers,
saved by sun-lamps and the proton beam.

So he thought we were on our way, not blithely
cresting the wave in gangshow singalongs
nor on the town with GI Joe and dames,
but modestly, always tipping his hat,
finding my second-hand bike, the best tinned fruit
we could afford, evap. or long-life cream,
my Sunday trousers always tailor-made.

I guess he was happiest in 1951:
the Nazis done and dusted, had paid their frigid tribute
in a tent at Lüneberg and Britain was *in festa*.
It was all contemporary: he was on the train
with just my Mum to see the Skylon
floating 50 feet above the ground,
the future he had always looked towards,
its rubric newly set in *sans-serif*,
everything discovered under just one dome,
dress-prints designed from crystallography!
Yet within the year modernity was scrappage,
down the river on Churchill's vengeful barge.

How much of the future can you expect?
Counting up he must have known Royal Art
was down the pan, that Mr. Aubrey,
trying to park what once was Peter Sellers'
Cadillac in Commerce Street, could not add up,
subtract, divide or multiply, found pots and plates

too heavy to carry over and dropped the lot.
He slipped away in just a Standard Ten,
to somewhere nice like Rhos-on-Sea
while my father, who could not bid chaos welcome,
walked to the old Exchange on Lockett's Lane,
back to the 'thirties, adding up his dole.

He left behind his medical dictionary, bookmarked
and underlined in red as though every sickness
could have its understanding and solution there,
every door he barred with reasons.
But chaos, wanting no handshake or by-your-leave
always finds a way to flick aside
the goodly dreams of old Arithmetic.

SEASCAPE (FROM HOLLY'S PHOTOGRAPH)

It is a desire – among so many others – to fuse
the blue of the sky, the blue of the sea,
and the blue haze between, into an oblong
of blue, blue and blue, each part bounded
but yet relieved of its old-time dismay.

It could be said how selfish is this act
because it leaves our life behind, or out;
so intent upon the oblong, so enamoured
of its purity, we might as well be saying:
'my mother is sick and I do not care.'

Unless it could be claimed the picture is in flight,
that to the desperate eye the oblong speaks
of all discomposure, that the teeming
in all air, light, and water is also
teeming here, just lashed down in pixel or pigment.

That may be how the oblong serves a true desire.
But if it is otherwise, if it is something
merely close to what it seems,
then its leaving us aside, we dabs of people,
need not be thoughtlessly or cruelly meant.

We are finite as we stand: the workman on a roof,
the watcher on the shore.   But when the silhouette
is no longer what we are, as we are shaded out,
stopped short of course of any leap to where
all circles straighten, all lines fuse,

we shall be glad – for as long as we can be –
that our mind can entertain no more
than blue, blue, and blue,
and it is by this faculty that we see where we are,
and out of what we came here, born alive.